More Of The Great Barrier Reef

Jennifer Murphy

Anne Price

This Book Belongs To

_____

Great Barrier Reef is wonderful.

It's up to us to save her.

Stop over-fishing. It's so harmful.

Then we will have it forever.

Coral Trout is sneaky you know.

Hiding deep down under the coral,

It waits for prey to come down low,

Camouflaged amongst the floral.

Spider Shell with its legs arranged,
its two eyes looking up at you.
A shell with eyes? That is so strange.
I've seen them, so I know it's true.

Sting Ray has such graceful wings.

It's closely related to sharks.

It's venomous, so watch its sting.

Hidden in its tail is a barb.

Pure white, small head,

with round black dots,

Barramundi Cod is a beauty.

It's endangered. There's not a lot.

Protect it now. That's our duty.

The **Lion Fish** is dangerous.

With its fins, it corners its prey.

The sting is filled with painfulness.

So be sure that you stay away.

Banded Coral Shrimp does its thing.
Cleans eel's teeth
while it opens wide,
Picking out rubbish 'til teeth gleam.
Good job the eel is on shrimp's side.

Black Tipped Reef Shark,

scary I bet.

It is not really all that large.

Usually doesn't pose a threat.

Annoying it, will make it charge.

We all love the **Clown Fish**, don't we?

It's protected from those who'd eat it.

Hiding amongst the anemone.

Perfect, you have to admit it.

Blue Tang Fish is very blue.

Its sharp spine is very spikey.

All day long on algae it chews.

Poison! For dinner, not likely.

Hammerhead Shark hunts
in the night,
Feeding on squid, crabs,
fish and rays.
Alone at night, it's a scary sight.
Swimming in schools
Throughout the day.

Giant Clam, with its luscious lips,

Filtering the sea water, so clever,

Taking out what is good to eat.

Living on the reef forever.

Loggerhead Turtle, a reptile,

Eats crabs, molluscs and jellyfish.

Left on their own when juvenile,

To tiger sharks,

they're a tasty dish.

Crown of Thorns is not very kind,
Sucking the life from the coral,
And leaving destruction behind.
It takes years to go back to normal.

Scientists are working with divers
To rid the reef of this pest.
Hope they can help the reef survive,
And bring it all back to its best.

Barracuda, so sharp its teeth,
Lurks in schools in amongst the reef.
Hunting smaller fish to eat.
Not a fish you would like to meet.

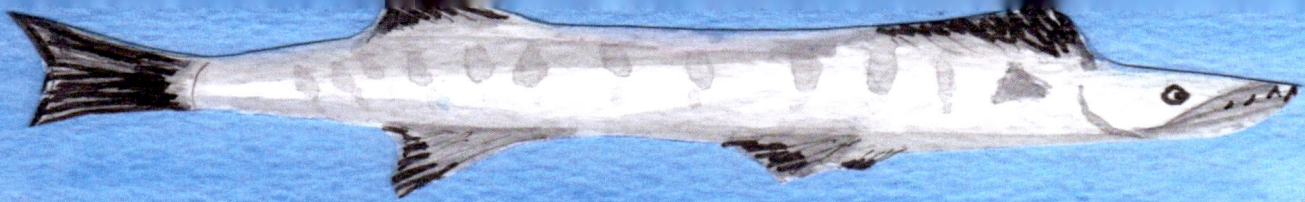

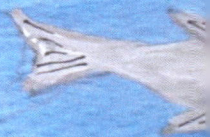

I'm a pretty Chinaman Fish,

I am a spectacular breed.

Poisonous if served in a dish.

If I am caught, I should be freed.

Spanish Mackerel are all stripey.

Great to eat for your fish and chips.

With lemon and salt by crikey.

Doesn't it make you lick your lips?

Parrot Fish have the strongest teeth.
They turn the coral into sand.
They really like eating reef.
We eat them, on the other hand.

Sea Urchins are covered

with spikes.

Sea Urchins don't have any eyes.

They see through their tubular feet,

Pretty shell hidden by disguise.

I'm the amazing Manta Ray.

Leaping out of water is my fun.

Removing parasites this way,

While jumping up out in the sun.

Bluebottle is a **Man of War**.

It's called this because of its looks.

A sail that carries it to the shore,

Ready to sting and make you crook.

I'm known as the **Painted Crayfish**.

I live in caves under the coral.

I'm a very sought after dish.

My colour is very floral.

Stinging Bream or **Happy Moment**,

Will spoil your day if you get hit.

Spines on its back, your opponent.

Handle with care and release it.

Sea Cucumbers

are strange creatures,

Not a food like the name suggests.

It has some very plain features.

I'll let you research the rest.

The fronds are waving in the sea.

Poison to almost all the fish.

Clown fish, friend of **Anemone**,

Safe from predators as they wish.

The **Humphead Moari Wrass**
is big.
It has a large hump on its head.
It grows much bigger than a pig.
Endangered! That's all to be said.

Geographic Cone is deadly.

Poisonous spikes, so do take care.

Don't pick it up so readily.

Know what it looks like. Be aware.

Dolphins are aquatic mammals.

A group of them is called a pod.

I guess you could say

they're man's pals.

You'll rarely catch them on a rod.

Irukandji and **Box Jelly**,
Like glass bubbles with tentacles,
Seek you out to sting your belly,
Ending up in your ventricles.

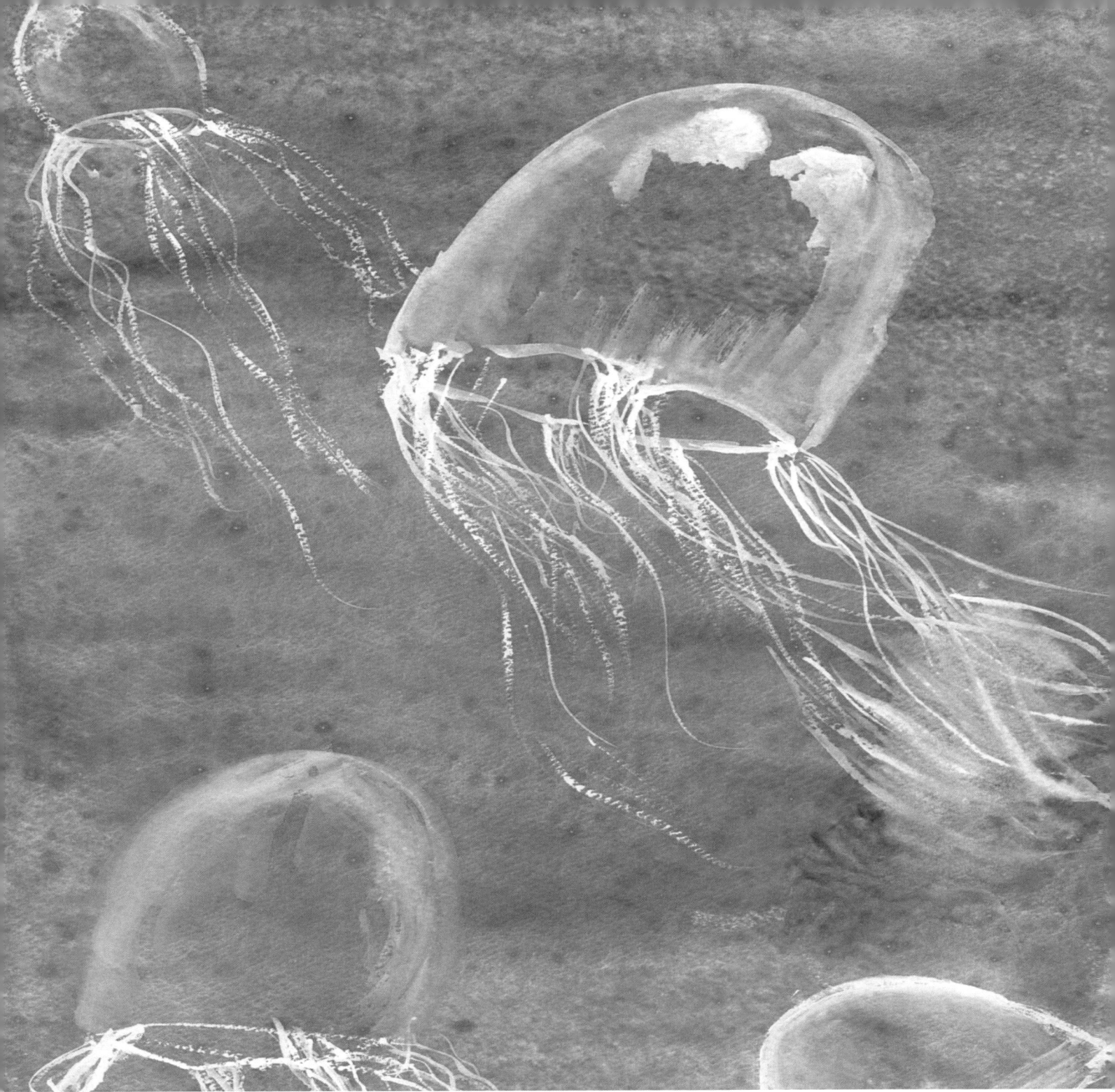

You think they don't enter the reef.

Think again because you are wrong.

Yes! **Crocodiles**, oh dear! Good grief!

They don't stay there for very long.

What has eight legs and googly eyes?

An Octopus I hear you say.

Such a clever one with disguise,

Changing colour to hide away.

Show off, that's what I like to do.

And the **Fire Fish** is my name.

Do not let my beauty fool you.

I am dangerous, like a flame.

Bright colours mean I'm nasty.
It's part of beauty on the reef.
Coral Stonefish, somewhat crafty,
Camouflaged, hoping you won't see.

The very eerie **Moray Eel**.

It eats octopus, fish and crabs.

Real sharp teeth that are

made like steel.

Stay away from them.

They will grab.

The Blue - Ringed Octopus

I am.

Don't let me fool you. I'm not kind.

Touch me and you are in a jam.

Nasty bite, I will leave behind.

Scorpion Fish, cute but unkind.

It hits with a kick when it pricks,

And stings with mucous

covered spines.

The pain will surely make you sick.

Flower Coral so heavenly.
Thing of beauty but
please take care.
Because it's dangerous and deadly,
Don't touch this. Just beware!

Tiger Shark! Not me!

No thank you.

Nasty but beautiful creatures.

Comes in from deep

where it is blue.

Its sharp teeth, a scary feature.

Spanish Dancer with frills galore.

Two horns like a garden grub.

Lots of colours, patterns and more

But its real name is a sea slug.

Wobbegong Shark, a night feeder,
On the reef buried in the grit.
Lots of pups at once, this breeder.
Hiding down in the sand it sits.

The **Potato Cod** is very rare,

Enjoying life in the water.

It's protected because we care.

We'll save this fish like we oughta!

Great White Shark. What a real beauty.
They are mostly seen in the deep.
I wouldn't say it's a cutie.
I know that it gives me the creeps.

The **Banded Sea Krait** is its name.

A sea snake but like no other.

On reef and on land is its fame.

Eats, comes on land to recover.

Like a small tree with legs,
Feathered Star,
Feeding down there it's not tethered.
Upside down it doesn't go far.
A starfish but it's like feathers.

To us the reef is very near.

So, as you can see, it's clear.

Plenty to see but lots to fear,

Perfect reef we all hold so dear.

Anne and Jennifer are a mother and

daughter team from Queensland, Australia.

Weekly get togethers creating art and

funny stories turned into an exciting new venture.

Their children's books are the result of

their life experiences and childhood memories.

The humour reflects how they like to

live- on the lighter side of life.

Follow us on Facebook at J & A kid's Books

www.ingramcontent.com/pod-product-compliance
Lightning Source LLC
Chambersburg PA
CBRC091536260326
41914CB00021B/1636